Excel 2024
Newer Functions

EASY EXCEL 2024 ESSENTIALS - BOOK 5

M.L. HUMPHREY

SELECT TITLES BY M.L. HUMPHREY

EXCEL 2024 ESSENTIALS
Excel 2024 for Beginners
Intermediate Excel 2024
Excel 2024 Useful Functions

EASY EXCEL 2024 ESSENTIALS
Formatting
Conditional Formatting
Charts
Pivot Tables
Newer Functions

See mlhumphrey.com for Microsoft Word, PowerPoint and Access titles and more

CONTENTS

CONTENTS (CONT.)

Introduction

This book is part of the *Easy Excel 2024 Essentials* series of titles. These are targeted titles that are excerpted from the main *Excel 2024 Essentials* series and are focused on one specific topic.

If you want a more general introduction to Excel, then you should check out the *Excel 2024 Essentials* titles instead; in this case, *Excel 2024 Useful Functions* which covers over fifty of the most useful functions available in Excel 2024.

But if you're already familiar with Excel and just want to learn a dozen of the more useful functions released in Excel 2016, Excel 2019, Excel 2021, and Excel 2024, then this is the book for you.

Excel Function Notation

For every function, Excel provides a text description of what the function does:

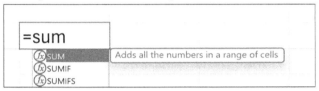

as well as a list of the inputs for that function:

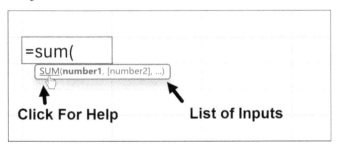

You can see above that the list of inputs for the SUM function are (number1, [number2], ...)

Any input that's in plain text, like number1, is required. Any input in brackets, like number2, is optional. The dot, dot, dot at the end of a list means you can add more of the same inputs if needed.

When a function has multiple inputs that require different types of information, like XLOOKUP, you have to provide the inputs in the correct order with each input separated by a comma.

As you work through creating a function, the portion that is bolded in the description at any given time is the input you are currently being asked to give to Excel.

The RANDBETWEEN Function

Notation: RANDBETWEEN(bottom, top)

Excel Definition: Returns a random number between the numbers you specify.

In writing this book, I have used RANDBETWEEN more times than I can count. Because what it does is lets you quickly and easily generate a series of whole numbers that fall within the range you specify. So that range of numbers for MIN and MAX? Generated by RANDBETWEEN. And the numbers used for SMALL and LARGE? Same.

RANDBETWEEN takes two inputs, the lowest possible number in the range, and the highest possible number in the range.

For example, if I want random numbers between 65 and 100, I would use:

=RANDBETWEEN(65,100)

and then copy that formula down however many rows I need.

Now, in that case, I wanted percentage values. So I had to write it as:

=RANDBETWEEN(65,100)/100

because RANDBETWEEN only generates whole number values.

RANDBETWEEN can also generate negative numbers.

For example,

=RANDBETWEEN(-100,100)

will generate random whole numbers between negative one hundred and positive one hundred.

It is possible that a value will repeat if you have a limited range of numbers. Each cell is its own formula. So each cell is randomly pulling a value from the range you gave it, independent of the other cells using that formula.

4

There is another function, RAND, that is similar to RANDBETWEEN, but what it returns is a random decimal value greater than 0 and less than 1 that is evenly distributed.

I never use it because I think I get the same result with something like:

$$=RANDBETWEEN(0,1000000)/1000000$$

If you do use RAND, it does not require any inputs. You just write it and then follow it with empty parens. For another example of a function that works like that, see the TODAY function, because I can't actually write the RAND function here. If I do, Word will turn it into a block of random text.

One final warning. The numbers you generate with RAND or RANDBETWEEN are *not static*. Every time you hit F9, use another formula, add text to a cell and hit Enter, etc., all of your randomly-generated values will generate again, and *you can't get the old numbers back*.

Undo does not work.

So if you are generating a list of random numbers that you want to do something with, turn them into fixed values before you do anything else.

I usually use paste special-values, but if you need to lock your result down immediately, type your formula in like normal, and then use F9 instead of Enter when you're done, and before you leave that cell.

That will use your formula to perform the calculation and also immediately convert the cell contents to the result. Use Enter, Tab, or click away to then leave the cell. (If you use Esc it will revert to the formula.)

To apply the F9 trick to an existing cell with a formula, click into the formula bar, use F2 after clicking on that cell or double-click on the cell, and then use F9.

Now let's discuss a new-to-me function, RANDARRAY, which is going to be our first array function.

The RANDARRAY Function

Notation: RANDARRAY([rows],[columns],[min],[max],[integer])

Excel Definition: Returns an array of random numbers.

One of the reasons I like writing these books is because it forces me to think through the various tools I use when working in Excel, and dig for better answers.

For example, just now when I was writing the RANDBETWEEN chapter, I thought, "I wonder if Excel has a function for generating a *range* of random numbers instead of doing it just one cell at a time like I do with RANDBETWEEN."

The answer was yes, RANDARRAY.

First off, let me tell you what an array function is. It's a function that can return results in more than one cell at a time. We haven't dealt with one of these yet. They're fairly new to Excel. I think it's only been the last three or four versions of Excel that have had them. The way they work has also changed over time. This is a book for Excel 2024, so I'm not going to get into how they used to work, but keep that in mind if you ever have to use an older version of Excel. You may have RANDARRAY available, but need to go to the Help function to see how to use it.

Okay. So.

First thing to note with RANDARRAY: Every single input to the function is listed in brackets, which means they are all optional. You can just write

$$=RANDARRAY()$$

and you will get a result. It will be the same result as if you'd used RAND: One cell with a decimal value between 0 and 1.

But RANDARRAY can do so much more than that.

The first input to the function is rows. The default value is 1. You can leave this input blank if you want one row of results. Or you can put a positive whole number which will tell Excel how many rows you want to populate with random values.

The second input is columns. It works the same as rows. Default is 1. If you only want one column of values, leave it blank. Otherwise put a positive whole number for the number of columns you want.

If you try to use a 0 for rows or columns, you will get a #CALC! error. If you try to use a negative value you will get a VALUE! error. So you either have to leave the inputs blank, or you have to put a positive whole number. (You can technically put a decimal, like 2.5, but Excel is just going to take the whole number portion and ignore the rest.)

The next two inputs to RANDARRY are min and max. This is the number range you want Excel to use when generating your random numbers. Leave those values blank and you'll get results between 0 and 1.

The final input, integer, is a TRUE/FALSE input. The default is FALSE, or 0, which will return decimal results. Put TRUE here (or the value 1) to get only integer results.

To use the default value for any input, just skip putting a value, and use a comma to indicate you're providing the next input. Here, for example, I have a RANDARRAY formula that will create a 2 by 2 grid of 0 and 1 values:

$$=RANDARRAY(2,2,,,1)$$

I used 2 for rows, 2 for columns, but then left min and max blank so that meant my range was going to be between 0 and 1. But then I put 1, TRUE, for my last input, which limited the result to whole numbers. That means in each of the four cells where Excel returns a value, the value will either be 1 or 0.

Here is another example:

$$=RANDARRAY(,4,1,10,TRUE)$$

This tells Excel to generate whole number values between 1 and 10 in four cells in a single row. Here is the result when the formula is in Cell A1:

A1			fx	=RANDARRAY(,4,1,10,TRUE)		
	A	B	C	D	E	F
1	8	7	7	8		
2						
3						
4						

A few more things to note about working with an array formula.

The formula goes in the first cell of the range where you want your values. So above, even though it gave me values in Cells A1 through D1, the formula I entered was entered into Cell A1.

When you're clicked away from cells that contain the results of an array formula, they look perfectly normal. It's only when you click onto them that you can see that the values were generated as part of an array function.

As you can see in the screenshot above, Excel puts a border around all of the cells that were populated using the array formula when you click on any cell in that range.

To edit an array formula, go to the top left cell of the range. The formula will show in the formula bar for any of the cells in the range, but will be grayed out for all but that top left cell.

Another thing to know about array functions is that they need enough room to work. You can't use an array function that takes up five rows by five columns if you already have text or values in that space. You'll get a #SPILL! error if there isn't enough room.

Every time you see #SPILL! that means that you are using an array function, and that the function doesn't have enough room to display its results. Either clear the contents of the cells that are blocking the formula, or move the formula to a cell where it has enough room. With RANDARRAY, you could also edit the formula to take up less space.

One more example before we move on. Here I nested RANDARRAY with decimal places within a ROUND function to generate a five-by-five table of currency values between 1 and 100:

$$=ROUND(RANDARRAY(5,5,1,100,FALSE),2)$$

This is what the result looks like:

	A	B	C	D	E	F	G
	C3		fx	=ROUND(RANDARRAY(5,5,1,100,FALSE),2)			
1	71.25	37.72	5.06	53.69	75.44		
2	75.8	80.69	31.34	5.4	86.56		
3	31.01	10.45	23.9	3.63	87.18		
4	52.2	78.34	1.28	56.33	18.71		
5	35.71	24.09	63.54	68	79.79		

Note that even though I am clicked into Cell C3, the formula you see is the one that was entered into Cell A1. Also, that the cells that are the result of the formula all have a border around the perimeter. And that the formula in the formula bar is grayed out because Cell C3 contains results from the formula, but not the formula itself.

One final note. RANDARRAY is a random-number-generating function, so be sure to lock down your values before you use your random numbers for any sort of calculation or demonstration that requires the numbers to stay fixed.

As I said before, I generally use paste special-values, but F9 did lock in the values for me here just in a unique way. It listed the values that were generated within a set of curly brackets in the first cell of the range. So =RANDARRAY(2,2,1,10,1) became ={9,4;2,8} and displayed the values 9, 4, 2, and 8 in a 2 by 2 range of cells.

The SUMIFS Function

Notation: SUMIFS(sum_range, criteria_range1, criteria1, …)

Excel Definition: Adds the cells specified by a given set of conditions or criteria.

This is one of my favorite functions. I use it all the time. What SUMIFS does is lets you apply SUM to a range of values if certain criteria are met. There is an older function, SUMIF, that let you do this for one single criteria, but if you master SUMIFS, you won't need it.

Okay, so let's look at the required inputs.

The first input is the range of cells where the values you want to add up are located.

The second input is the first range of cells that contain information you want to evaluate. It can be the same range of cells as the ones you want to sum. Later, for example, I have a formula for determining the total value of purchases over $100.

The third input is your criteria you want to apply to that range of cells.

For this function that … at the end is important to understand. Because if you keep going, you need to actually add two additional inputs at a time. The next input you'd put there is the *second* range of cells that you want to evaluate. But you'd also then need to provide a fifth input, which is the criteria to use on that second range of cells.

This is what that would look like written out in notation format:

SUMIFS(sum_range, criteria_range1, criteria1, criteria_range2, criteria2,…)

The maximum number of criteria you can have is 127, although why you would ever want to do that, I do not know. That would be way too prone to error in my opinion.

Speaking of errors. If your cell ranges are not the same size for each range input (sum_range and each criteria_range), you will get a #VALUE! error. Excel needs to know what to match up.

I've only ever used SUMIFS (or any of the similar functions that we'll discuss next) with a table of data where my input ranges were in columns. But I did just try it with rows, and that worked, too. You can also use something like a 2x3 cell range, but all of your range inputs would then need to be 2x3 as well. The ranges always have to match up.

Your criteria can look at numeric values, dates, or text. You can also combine different types of criteria in the same function.

For example, I can have Excel sum transactions that occurred in 2024 (a date criteria), were over $100 (a number criteria), and involved customers in Alaska (a text criteria).

Let's now talk about how to write each of those properly.

For a number, you can either just write the number (22) or use quote marks around the number ("22").

For a greater than (>), less than (<), greater than or equal to (>=), or less than or equal to (<=) criteria, you need to put the whole expression in quotes. So greater than or equal to 22, would be ">=22" in that part of the function.

To evaluate dates, you also need to put them in quotes. So "7/23/2020" or "7/23/20" both work. If all else fails, convert the date you want to a number (44035 in this case), and write it that way, but you shouldn't have to do that.

It is possible to combine dates with the greater than and less than symbols as well. For example using ">5/1/2020" would look for any entry in the range after May 1, 2020.

You can also use cell references if the value you want is in a cell. (This is very useful for something like counting the number of sales per state. Create a list of all state abbreviations, write a formula that references the first entry in that list, use fixed cell references for your table or reference the entire column, and then just copy that formula down for all the states.)

To use greater than, less than, etc. with a cell reference, you have to write it as ">"& and then the cell reference. So

$$">"\&G25$$

would be how you write greater than the value in Cell G25.

To evaluate text, put it in quotes. So, "Alaska" would look for entries in that cell range for Alaska.

With text you can also use wildcards. An asterisk (*) represents any number of characters or spaces. So if I write

$$"*e*"$$

as my criteria, that would look for any entry that contains the letter e.

If I instead looked for

$$"e*"$$

that would look for any entry that *starts* with the letter e. And if I used

$$"*e"$$

that would look for any entry that *ends* with the letter e.

The other available wildcard is the question mark (?), which represents one single character, including a single space.

So if I looked for

"??e"

that would return any three-letter entry that ends in e.

But keep in mind that each question mark is a character/space so "??e" would not capture the entry "be" since it is only two letters.

Also. If you ever want to use text that includes an actual asterisk or a question mark in your criteria, precede the asterisk or question mark with a tilde (~).

Okay. Time to look at some examples. Here is our data:

	A	B	C	D	E
1	Date	Customer Name	Product	Units	Total Cost
2	2/6/2020	Lee	Widget	14	$ 31.50
3	2/25/2020	Morales	Whatchamacallit	3	$ 33.75
4	4/1/2020	Jones	Widget	8	$ 18.00
5	4/7/2020	Jones	Whatchamacallit	11	$ 123.75
6	4/25/2020	Phong	Whatsit	11	$ 14.85
7	4/28/2020	Gutierrez	Widget	9	$ 20.25
8	5/2/2020	Holsen	Whatchamacallit	24	$ 270.00
9	5/4/2020	Morales	Whatsit	15	$ 20.25
10	5/6/2020	Gutierrez	Whatsit	1	$ 1.35
11	5/26/2020	Lee	Whatchamacallit	3	$ 33.75
12	6/10/2020	Smith	Whatchamacallit	4	$ 9.00
13	6/12/2020	Smith	Whatsit	2	$ 2.70
14	7/11/2020	Holsen	Widget	6	$ 13.50
15	7/18/2020	Phong	Whatchamacallit	9	$ 101.25
16	7/23/2020	Fromer	Whatsit	11	$ 14.85
17					

We have date of transaction, customer last name, product, units bought, and total cost.

I want to answer the following questions using this data:

1. How much did customer Lee spend?

2. How much did customer Lee spend on or after May 1, 2020?

3. What was the total value of purchases over $100?

4. How many What-type products did customer Smith purchase?

Take a moment and think about how you'd do that. And then look here at how I did it:

Question	Formula	Result
How much did customer Lee spend?	=SUMIFS(E2:E16,B2:B16,"Lee")	$ 65.25
How much did customer Lee spend on or after May 1, 2020?	=SUMIFS(E2:E16,B2:B16,"Lee",A2:A16,">=5/1/2020")	$ 33.75
What was the total value of purchases over $100?	=SUMIFS(E2:E16,E2:E16,">100")	$ 495.00
How many What-type products did customer Smith purchase?	=SUMIFS(D2:D16,C2:C16,"What*",B2:B16,"Smith")	6

The first question was "How much did customer Lee spend?" Which means we want to sum the cost column, and we have one criteria to apply, that the customer last name be Lee.

Here that is:

$$=SUMIFS(E2:E16,B2:B16,"Lee")$$

Note here that our criteria was text, so Lee is in quotes.

The next question takes that first example and limits it with a second criteria to purchases made on or after May 1, 2020. Adding that to our formula we get:

$$=SUMIFS(E2:E16,B2:B16,"Lee",A2:A16,">=5/1/2020")$$

Note that the >= and the date itself are all in quotes together.

Now let's look at the third question, "What was the total value of purchases over $100?" With this one, the criteria range and the sum range are the same:

$$=SUMIFS(E2:E16,E2:E16,">100")$$

It also uses a greater than symbol with a number, so both have to be included in quotes. Another option would be:

$$=SUMIFS(E2:E16,E2:E16,">"\&100)$$

where we join the greater than symbol to the number using an ampersand.

The fourth question is "How many what-type products did customer Smith purchase?"

To solve this one, we have to think about our product types. We have Whatsits, Widgets, and Whatchamacallits. Two of those are "what-type" products, Whatsits and Whatchamacallits.

The simplest solution is to use the wildcard asterisk character to get our answer:

$$=SUMIFS(D2:D16,C2:C16,"What*",B2:B16,"Smith")$$

By using "What*" I captured both products. (Note that Excel is not case-sensitive with text criteria so it views what and What as the same.)

Another option would be:

$$=SUM(SUMIFS(D2:D16,C2:C16,\{"Whatsit","Whatchamacallit"\},B2:B16,"Smith"))$$

Note that I used curly brackets to create a list for that particular input. And that because the list didn't use the plural of each product name, I had to be careful to use "Whatsit" instead of "Whatsits" and "Whatchamacallit" instead of "Whatchamacallits".

Also, it required SUM around the SUMIFS function, because otherwise it returns separate results in separate cells for Whatsit and Whatchamacallit.

Finally, note that this last example used a different sum range (Column D), because we were adding up units this time rather than amount made.

One final thought, I always like to test things like this on on a small range of my data where I can also manually compute the answer. That lets me confirm that the result my formula returns is what I'd expect.

One mistake I often make when initially writing a formula or filter or anything else involving numbers, is that I will write it as "greater than" or "less than" when what I really want is "greater than or equal to" or "less than or equal to". So I always try to test my edge cases. For example, with the $100 or more question, I'd use fake data that included values of 99.99, 100, and 100.01 to see if the result matched my expectations.

The other things I check for if I get an error message or my formula isn't working as expected, is that my quotes, commas, and cell ranges are where and what they should be.

The COUNTIFS Function

Notation: COUNTIFS(criteria_range1, criteria1, …)

Excel Definition: Counts the number of cells specified by a given set of conditions or criteria.

Where SUMIFS sums values based on the criteria you give it, COUNTIFS counts them. Despite the name, the type of count function used here is COUNTA, which, if you recall, counts more than just numbers. (This is good, actually, I just mention it lest there be confusion.)

Note that since COUNTIFS is just counting results, it doesn't require that first input that SUMIFS does. It jumps right into the criteria ranges.

Also, just like SUMIFS has SUMIF, there is a COUNTIF function that can be used for one criteria. You can actually turn a COUNTIF function into a COUNTIFS function just by adding an S to the function name. (You can't do this with SUMIF and SUMIFS because the inputs are in a different order.)

In terms of building a COUNTIFS function, most of what you need to know was already discussed in the SUMIFS chapter. They handle criteria in the exact same way. So let's just dive in and walk through some questions we can answer with COUNTIFS.

Using the same data from the SUMIFS chapter, how would you answer the following questions:

1. How many transactions were there for customer Phong?

2. How many purchases did customer Phong make of Whatchamacallits?

3. How many purchases of more than ten units were made in April 2020?

4. How many purchases of Widgets and Whatsits were made?

Let's start with the first one: "How many transactions were there for customer Phong?" You just need Column B for this one, right?

If you did this manually, you would look down Column B, and every time it says "Phong", you would count that entry. Written as a formula it looks like this:

=COUNTIFS(B:B,"Phong")

The next question, "How many purchases of Whatchamacallits did customer Phong make?" takes that initial count but refines it to only transactions in Whatchamacallits.

That requires two pieces of information, customer name and product. As a formula it looks like this:

=COUNTIFS(B:B,"Phong",C:C,"Whatchamacallit")

(Note here that I'm using the entire columns for my cell ranges. I have nothing below my data table, so I can get away with that.)

The next question is a bit trickier: "How many purchases of more than ten units were made in April 2020?"

The first part is easy enough, it's just using the Units column and looking for any value greater than ten. But stop and think about what it means to be in April 2020. Clearly you need to use the Date column, but how would you write that?

Here's what I ended up doing:

=COUNTIFS(D:D,">10",A:A,">=4/1/2020",A:A,"<5/1/20")

I used two criteria on the same column. The date needed to be on or after April 1, 2020, that's the first criteria I used, and also before May 1, 2020, that's the second criteria I used.

Was is the most elegant and streamlined solution? Maybe not. But on something simple like this, "if it works, it works" is a good approach to take. When you're dealing with 15 rows of data you can be a bit clunky.

Okay. Final one: How many purchases of Widgets and Whatsits were made?

We can't use the wildcard symbol like we did in the last chapter, so we need to come up with another approach. This is the one I came up with:

=COUNTIFS(C:C,"Widget")+COUNTIFS(C:C,"Whatsit")

And it worked.

But as you may recall from the SUMIFS chapter, I could have also used:

=SUM(COUNTIFS(C:C,{"Widget","Whatsit"}))

Let's explore what happens when I don't surround that with SUM.

On the next page is a screenshot of a table I created with my product names in Column H. In Cell I2, I put the following formula:

=COUNTIFS(C:C,H2:H4)

That returns an array result. Excel filled Cells I2 through I4 with the count for each product type itself.

I didn't have to copy a formula to get this result, Excel just did it.

Pretty interesting, huh?

The AVERAGEIFS Function

Notation: AVERAGEIFS(average_range, criteria_range1, criteria1, …)

Excel Definition: Finds average (arithmetic mean) for the cells specified by a given set of conditions or criteria.

AVERAGEIFS works much like SUMIFS, except it is looking for the average of the values that meet the specified criteria.

This uses the AVERAGE function, not the AVERAGEA function, so the values you want to average have to be numbers or dates. If you try to apply it to a range of values that are all TRUE/FALSE or text values, it will return a #DIV/0! error.

If the range has numbers in it as well as TRUE/FALSE and/or text values, it will only average the number results. (Which means be careful that the range of values you use are all actually numbers since it won't look at any numbers stored as text.)

(Also, you can use it with dates, which are technically numbers. It will give you a date that's within the range of the dates that meet your criteria, I'm just not quite sure how you'd interpret the result.)

There is an AVERAGEIF function, but if you master AVERAGEIFS you won't need to use it.

Since at this point I think you have the general gist of how each of these functions work, let's just look at a few examples.

First, using the data table we used for SUMIFS and COUNTIFS, how would you calculate the average amount customers spent per transaction when they bought Whatsits?

This requires looking at Total Cost based on only one criteria, product. The formula is:

$$=AVERAGEIFS(E2:E16,C2:C16,"Whatsit")$$

What if we wanted that same calculation, but for all three product types? Just like with COUNTIFS, it turns out we can do this with an array:

12		☰ ✕ ✓ *fx*	=AVERAGEIFS(E:E,C:C,H2:H4)		

	H	I	J
1	**Product**	**Average Spent**	
2	Whatsit	$ 10.80	
3	Widget	$ 20.81	
4	Whatchamacallit	$ 95.25	
5			

In this case I put

$$=AVERAGEIFS(E:E,C:C,H2:H4)$$

into Cell I2, and it populated the values for Cells I2 through I4.

Finally, how would you write a formula to calculate the average amount customers spent per transaction on Whatsits in June? I wrote it like this:

=AVERAGEIFS(E2:E16,C2:C16,"Whatsit",A2:A16,">=6/1/2020",A2:A16,"<7/1/20")

The MINIFS Function

Notation: MINIFS(min_range, criteria_range1, criteria1, ...)

Excel Definition: Returns the minimum value among cells specified by a given set of conditions or criteria.

MINIFS gives you the minimum value within a range of cells that meet your chosen criteria. There is not a corresponding MINIF function.

MINIFS uses the same type of criteria that we discussed in detail in the SUMIFS chapter, and it will also return an array of values for you like we showed in the SUMIFS, COUNTIFS, and AVERAGEIFS chapters.

Here is an example of results using both MINIFS and MAXIFS to get minimum and maximum spend per transaction for each customer:

Customer	Min Spent in One Transaction	Max Spent in One Transaction
Fromer	$ 14.85	$ 14.85
Gutierrez	$ 1.35	$ 20.25
Holsen	$ 13.50	$ 270.00
Jones	$ 18.00	$ 123.75
Lee	$ 31.50	$ 33.75
Morales	$ 20.25	$ 33.75
Phong	$ 14.85	$ 101.25
Smith	$ 2.70	$ 9.00

This was built with just two formulas:

=MINIFS(E:E,B:B,H2:H9)

in Cell I2 (the second cell in the second column). And in Cell J2:

=MAXIFS(E:E,B:B,H2:H9)

One new little thing to point out for this chapter: If you get results like I did here using an array (the H2:H9 part of each of those formulas), you can't then sort that table of data by the results.

When I first did this one, I had the customer names in random order based on what Remove Duplicates gave me. After I added my MINIFS formula using an array, I tried to sort it alphabetically. It wouldn't let me.

There are two ways to fix that. One is to paste special-values for that table now that the results are there, and then sort.

The other option, which is what I did, was to move the two cells that have the formulas in them to somewhere else for a moment, sort the customer names in the table, and then bring those two formulas back.

Your other option, of course, is to not use an array in the formula. Just write the formulas in Cells I2 and J2 with a reference to H2 only, and then copy the formulas down.

You can still filter a table using an array result without issues. It seems to just be the Sort option that's affected.

The MAXIFS Function

Notation: MAXIFS(max_range, criteria_range1, criteria1, …)

Excel Definition: Returns the maximum value among cells specified by a given set of conditions or criteria.

MAXIFS is our final [Function]IFS function, and it takes the maximum from a range of specified cells based on your criteria. By now you hopefully know how that works. If not, go read the SUMIFS chapter and just think "maximum" instead of "sum" everywhere.

Like MINIFS, it does not have a corresponding single criteria function. (This is because by the time they created the MINIFS and MAXIFS functions they had not gotten around to creating a MINIF or MAXIF function yet, so one was never needed.)

In the MINIFS chapter, you can see an example of MAXIFS applied to the data table we've been working with, and looking at transaction amount for each customer.

In this chapter I wanted to bring it all together with a new example that uses COUNTIFS, AVERAGEIFS, MINIFS, and MAXIFS.

On the next page we have a table of test scores for eighteen students in Professor Jones's class. I want to know if there's any difference between how males and females perform:

I'm using arrays here. That means the formula for MAXIFS in Cell I2 is

$$=MAXIFS(\$A\$2:\$A\$19,\$B\$2:\$B\$19,\$E\$2:\$E\$3)$$

Note that I used \$ signs to fix the references to the data table and to the two values I wanted to evaluate. I did that so I could copy the formula in Cell F2 to Cells G2, H2, and I2, and only have to adjust the function name. (I am very lazy, sometimes to the point of creating more work for myself.)

What did that tell us?

We have 8 men and 10 women in the class. The average class score for men is 79 and for women is 94. The range for men is 70 to 94. The range for women is 89 to 100.

	A	B	C	D	E	F	G	H	I
1	Score	Gender	Professor			COUNT	AVERAGE	MIN	MAX
2	100	Female	Jones		Male	8	79.125	70	94
3	89	Male	Jones		Female	10	94.2	89	100
4	98	Female	Jones						
5	89	Male	Jones						
6	70	Male	Jones						
7	70	Male	Jones						
8	71	Male	Jones						
9	90	Female	Jones						
10	80	Male	Jones						
11	70	Male	Jones						
12	89	Female	Jones						
13	89	Female	Jones						
14	91	Female	Jones						
15	97	Female	Jones						
16	94	Male	Jones						
17	95	Female	Jones						
18	100	Female	Jones						
19	93	Female	Jones						
20									

It looks like we have a difference there. Just be careful coming to a conclusion as to why. We don't know if that's the teacher's bias, or maybe this class meets at eight in the morning, and there are four male students who are good friends in the class who really like to party on Thursday nights, and end up missing Friday's quizzes.

The TEXTJOIN Function

Notation: TEXTJOIN(delimiter, ignore_empty, text1, …)

Excel Definition: Concatenates a list or range of text strings using a delimiter.

TEXTJOIN is a newer function, but it's one I've come to love. (For some reason I can love Excel functions and pets much more easily than humans. Go figure.)

Anyway. What it does is it takes text inputs and joins them into a single entry. You can tell it how to separate those entries with what you provide as the delimiter(s).

You can also tell it how to deal with empty fields so that you don't run into the issue I mentioned with CONCATENATE where you get an extra space and need to use TRIM to clean it up.

Here is our data table and result:

	A	B	C	D	E	F
1	First Name	Middle Initial	Last Name	Suffix	Full Name	Formula
2	John		Lee	Jr.	John Lee Jr.	=TEXTJOIN(" ",TRUE,A2:D2)
3	Sarah	J.	Morales		Sarah J. Morales	=TEXTJOIN(" ",TRUE,A3:D3)
4	Lee	K.	Jones	Esq.	Lee K. Jones Esq.	=TEXTJOIN(" ",TRUE,A4:D4)
5	Ann		Phong		Ann Phong	=TEXTJOIN(" ",TRUE,A5:D5)
6	Jose	A.	Gutierrez		Jose A. Gutierrez	=TEXTJOIN(" ",TRUE,A6:D6)
7	Dean		Holsen		Dean Holsen	=TEXTJOIN(" ",TRUE,A7:D7)
8	Francisco	R.	Morales		Francisco R. Morales	=TEXTJOIN(" ",TRUE,A8:D8)
9	Marney	B.	Smith		Marney B. Smith	=TEXTJOIN(" ",TRUE,A9:D9)
10	Kelly		Fromer		Kelly Fromer	=TEXTJOIN(" ",TRUE,A10:D10)
11						

Columns A through D have the text we want to join together.

Column E is the result of using this TEXTJOIN formula in Row 2 and copying it down:

$$=TEXTJOIN(" ",TRUE,A2:D2)$$

Column F shows the formula for each row.

Now let's break that down.

The first input is the delimiter. This is just a fancy way of saying "what is between the entries". The delimiter I used is a single space. I had to put it into quotes since I typed it directly into the function.

The second input is a TRUE/FALSE input where you tell Excel whether to ignore empty cells or not. Since I don't want those weird extra spaces when a middle name or suffix is missing, I put TRUE. If I had said FALSE, there wouldn't be any text to put there, but Excel would include the delimiter, and I'd end up with two spaces next to each other or an extra one at the end.

Finally, the third input is for text. Excel lets you list each text reference individually, separated by a comma. But it also let me use a cell range since my inputs were in the order I wanted: A2:D2.

This would also work, it just takes a little more effort to create:

=TEXTJOIN(" ",TRUE,A2,B2,C2,D2)

If the resulting text string is too long (32,767 characters) Excel will return a #VALUE! error.

TEXTJOIN is very easy to use compared to CONCATENATE or CONCAT, which is how I would've done this before. With those functions, you have to list the delimiter as a separate entry each time, so you have A2," ",B2," ", etc. all the way down the line.

Based on that difference, you might think CONCATENATE (I never used CONCAT but it was the shortened name they came out with at some point) is the way to go if you want to use different delimiters, because you can manually add each one as you create your text string.

But it turns out that TEXTJOIN also lets you have multiple delimiters.

You have two options.

First, you can include them in the function itself by using curly brackets around your list of delimiters, putting each one in quotes, and separating them with a comma. Here, for example, I have space, space, and then a comma with a space:

=TEXTJOIN({" "," ",", "},TRUE,A16:D16)

It's a little hard to read after the fact, but pretty easy to create.

Second, you can put your delimiters into cells, like I did on the next page in Cells G20 to G22. Cells G20 and G21 have spaces, Cell G22 has a comma and a space.

If you do that, you can then reference that cell range as your first input. For example, the formula I used in Cell G16 was:

=TEXTJOIN($G$20:$G$22,TRUE,A16:D16)

Note that I put $ signs on the cell references for the first input. That lets me copy the formula to other cells while still referencing the range of cells with my delimiters in them.

	A	B	C	D	G	H
15	**First Name**	**Middle Initial**	**Last Name**	**Suffix**	**Full Name**	**Formula**
16	John		Lee	Jr.	John Lee Jr.	=TEXTJOIN($G$20:$G$22,TRUE,A16:D16)
17	Lee	K.	Jones	Esq.	Lee K. Jones, Esq.	=TEXTJOIN($G$20:$G$22,TRUE,A17:D17)
18						
19					**Delimiters**	**Description**
20						Space
21						Space
22					,	Comma, Space
23						

Now. We have a problem. Look at the values in Cells G16 and G17. G17 is great and perfect and wonderful. Lee K. Jones, Esq. is exactly what we wanted. But John Lee Jr. is not. Why?

Because it turns out that if you give Excel more than one delimiter to use, it will go to that list of delimiters only when it needs one. So what happened here for John Lee Jr. is that it needed a delimiter between John and Lee, so grabbed that first space. Then I told it to skip the middle initial if it was empty, so it did. When it needed another delimiter to put between Lee and Jr., it grabbed the next delimiter in the list, which was the second one, a space.

You might think that the way to solve this is to change that TRUE to a FALSE and surround the whole thing with TRIM. But no. That doesn't work. You end up with a comma at the end of all of the entries that don't have a suffix. (How do I know? I tried it. It's always good to experiment in Excel and see what you get.)

As of now, I think the best way to solve this would be an IFS function (which we discuss later in the book) where you'd use a conditional statement that said "(a) if there's no suffix, then use a space and skip blanks, (b) but if there is a suffix, then don't skip anything and use this list of delimiters but trim out extra spaces".

=IFS(ISBLANK(D3),TEXTJOIN("
",TRUE,A3:D3),TRUE,TRIM(TEXTJOIN($G$20:$G$22,FALSE,A3:D3)))

It looks ugly, and uses ISBLANK, which is another function we haven't covered that just asks if a cell is blank or not, but I think it works.

Break that down and we have these two TEXTJOIN functions:

TEXTJOIN(" ",TRUE,A3:D3)

TRIM(TEXTJOIN($G$20:$G$22,FALSE,A3:D3))

Since we used TRUE in the first one, we don't need TRIM. But since we used FALSE for the second one, any time there is a missing middle initial we'd have a double space without TRIM, so we need it.

(That was fun for me, but probably not for you. Just let it sit there for now as one of those things Excel can do if you are willing to explore and experiment to find a solution.)

Okay.

One more thing to know about delimiters. If you use a list of different delimiters, and Excel needs more than the list you gave it, Excel will circle back to the start of your list. So be sure you've thought through the different iterations of your results and how those will work with the delimiters you've provided if you're going to provide more than one delimiter.

The **TEXTBEFORE** Function

Notation: TEXTBEFORE(text, delimiter, [instance_num], [match_mode], [match_end], [if_not_found])

Excel Definition: Returns text that's before delimiting characters.

They make this look really complicated, don't they? But really it's just a big fancy function to say "I want the text that falls before this other text."

Note that the only required inputs are the text and the delimiter. All the rest is optional.

So let's go back to Cell A2 with its entry of "$10 dollars" from the last chapter.

If I want to extract the dollar sign and number, so drop the part that says " dollars", I can just write:

=TEXTBEFORE(A2," dollars")

For me personally, it's easier to understand what I'm telling it to do to use " dollars", but that doesn't mean I can't simplify it down later. I could actually use:

=TEXTBEFORE(A2," ")

That tells Excel to pull everything before the first space. Since there is only one space in the entry, it's that simple.

Okay. So that is TEXTBEFORE at its most basic. Your first input is the text or cell reference where the text is. Your second input is where in that text to draw the line.

But you can get fancier.

The third input is instance_num. Sometimes you'll have a text string and want to remove the text before a certain point, but maybe the delimiter you want to use for that is one that appears earlier in that text string, too.

Here is an example:

	A	B	C
8	**Value**	**Isolate Name**	**Formula**
9	John Lee Investigator	John Lee	=TEXTBEFORE(A9," ",2)
10	Lee Jones Lawyer	Lee Jones	=TEXTBEFORE(A10," ",2)
11	Kelly Fromer Teacher	Kelly Fromer	=TEXTBEFORE(A11," ",2)
12			

I have three listings where the information is first name, space, last name, space, profession. To isolate just the name in Cell A9, I can use:

$$=TEXTBEFORE(A9," ",2)$$

That's saying, "Look at the text in Cell A9, find the second space, and bring back everything before that point".

If the text entries had been something like "Kelly Fromer, Teacher" then we'd need to use a comma and a space as our delimiter:

$$=TEXTBEFORE(A13,", ")$$

Of course, as you may remember when we were using TEXTJOIN, data isn't always that neat and tidy. You may have variation in the number of spaces in different cells.

It turns out, your instance number can also be a negative number.

If you do that, Excel will start at the end instead of the beginning of your text. So with entries like, "Joseph L. Jones, Jr., Teacher" and "Daphne Clark, Astronaut" I'd use:

$$=TEXTBEFORE(A21,",",-1)$$

That looks for a comma delimiter, but it does it from the end, so I don't end up dropping the suffix from someone's name. (I don't need to include the space after the comma in the delimiter, because we're pulling everything to the left of the comma. I could use it, but it's not needed.)

The match_mode input lets you say whether Excel should be case-sensitive when it looks for the delimiter.

This was another one that I had a hard time thinking up an example for, but with my Google book links, I'll often add &gl= and then the two letter country abbreviation at the end to link to Google stores in different countries. So let's say I was trying to extract a website address that didn't have that on the end. TEXTBEFORE is one way I could do that.

Here we go:

	A	B	C
13	**Website***	**Case-Sensitive**	**Formula**
14	www.Abs&Glutes.com&gl=AU	www.Abs&Glutes.com	=TEXTBEFORE(A14,"&gl",,0)
15		**Not Case-Sensitive**	**Formula**
16		www.Abs	=TEXTBEFORE(A14,"&gl",,1)
17			
18	*Completely made up - do not blame me if it's real and weird.		
19			

This (made up) website address, Abs&Glutes.com, includes &Gl in the name. If I don't tell Excel to treat my delimiter, &gl, as case-sensitive, Excel won't pull the full website address for me.

The formula I need is:

$$=TEXTBEFORE(A14,"\&gl",,0)$$

where that 0 in the last position tells Excel to treat &gl separate from &Gl.

Another thing to note about the formula I used here is that I didn't need the instance_num input, so I just left it blank. If you're not comfortable doing that, you could also use:

$$=TEXTBEFORE(A14,"\&gl",1,0)$$

The next optional input is match_end, which according to Excel "treats the end of text as a delimiter". I went to the help text to understand what this meant, but it was not in fact helpful.

I think I know what this is for, though. If you use a delimiter that isn't contained in the text in that cell—so a comma when the cell has no commas—Excel is going to by default generate a #N/A error as your result. But if you put 1 for this input, Excel will instead return the full text in the cell.

If you want something else returned instead of the full text or #N/A, that's where the final input, if_not_found, can be used. It only gets used if the input before it for match_end is 0 or blank, *and* there is no match to the delimiter.

You can use a number for this input. Excel will return that number as text. If you want to put actual text, be sure to surround the text with quote marks.

Here is an example with text:

$$=TEXTBEFORE(A23,",",,0,0,"Nothing There")$$

I suspect you'll only use the last two optional inputs when you're getting some sort of error in your results that needs to be overcome by suppressing the #N/A error, which can interfere in certain calculations.

The other time you may see a #N/A error for this function is if the instance_num you use is greater than the number of times the delimiter occurs in the text.

You may also see a #VALUE! error if the instance_num you use is a larger number than the length of the text in the cell. So, for example, 4 in a cell that only has the word "ten".

You will also see that if you list zero for the instance_num.

Okay, that was kind of fun to explore, let's now look at its counterpart, TEXTAFTER.

The TEXTAFTER Function

Notation: TEXTAFTER(text, delimiter, [instance_num], [match_mode], [match_end], [if_not_found])

Excel Definition: Returns the text that's after delimiting characters.

TEXTAFTER is the counterpart to TEXTBEFORE. They actually have the exact same inputs, it's just which side of the delimiter you return.

Let's revisit two of our examples from the TEXTBEFORE chapter:

	A	B	C
8	**Value**	**Isolate Profession**	**Formula**
9	John Lee Investigator	Investigator	=TEXTAFTER(A9," ",2)
10	Lee Jones Lawyer	Lawyer	=TEXTAFTER(A10," ",2)
11	Kelly Fromer Teacher	Teacher	=TEXTAFTER(A11," ",2)
12			
13	**Value**	**Isolate Profession**	**Formula**
14	Joseph L. Jones, Jr., Teacher	Teacher	=TEXTAFTER(A14,", ",-1)
15	Daphne Clark, Astronaut	Astronaut	=TEXTAFTER(A15,", ",-1)
16			

In Rows 9 through 11 I had first name, last name, profession, all separated by a single space. To get the profession from those cells, all I had to do was change my TEXTBEFORE formula that extracted the names to TEXTAFTER:

$$=TEXTAFTER(A9," ",2)$$

This formula looks in Cell A9, finds the second space, and brings back everything after that.

In Rows 14 and 15 we have profession separated out with a comma and a space, but there's also a name with a comma and a space before the suffix.

Fortunately, I can use a delimiter that is a comma and space combined, and then a -1 for instance_num to pull profession:

$$=\text{TEXTAFTER(A14,", ",-1)}$$

Just like with TEXTBEFORE, the match_mode input is used to determine if the delimiter should be case-sensitive. Match_end is used to return the entire cell contents instead of an #N/A result when there's no match to the delimiter, and if_not_found is used to return a custom result instead of #N/A or the entire cell contents.

One final example for you.

In the MID chapter, we wanted to extract just the number from entries like $123 dollars and $1234 dollars. You can also do that using a combination of TEXTBEFORE and TEXTAFTER. Specifically:

$$=\text{TEXTBEFORE(TEXTAFTER(A2,"\$")," ")}$$

That says, "take text after the dollar sign and then, from that result, take the text from before the first space".

It might be easier to understand written as:

$$=\text{TEXTBEFORE(TEXTAFTER(A2,"\$")," dollars")}$$

But that limits it to entries that use dollars, whereas the first example would work with a variety of currencies.

Also, for the bored overachievers, it turns out you can give Excel a list of delimiters to use with these ones, too.

Here I have a variety of currency entries, and I want to remove the currency symbol from before all of them. I can do that with a TEXTAFTER formula:

	A	B	C
17	Value	Remove Currency Symbol	Formula
18	$10 dollars	10 dollars	=TEXTAFTER(A18,{"$","£","€"})
19	£123 pounds	123 pounds	=TEXTAFTER(A19,{"$","£","€"})
20	€1234 euros	1234 euros	=TEXTAFTER(A20,{"$","£","€"})
21	€1234 euros, $10 dollars, £123 pounds	1234 euros, $10 dollars, £123 pounds	=TEXTAFTER(A21,{"$","£","€"})
22	$10 dollars, £123 pounds, €1234 euros	10 dollars, £123 pounds, €1234 euros	=TEXTAFTER(A22,{"$","£","€"})

Look at Rows 18 to 20. What I did here is used curly brackets around the different delimiters I wanted Excel to use.

$$=\text{TEXTAFTER(A18,\{"\$","£","€"\})}$$

It looked for each delimiter and then when it found one of them, extracted the text past that point. Pretty cool, huh?

But now look at Rows 21 and 22 where it didn't work so well. Note that it stopped as soon as there was a match to any delimiter, so you can't extract all of the currency symbols this way.

Based on the results in those rows, I think Excel starts at the first character and goes through its list looking for each delimiter you give it. If there's a hit on a delimiter, it will give you all the text after that point. If not, it goes to the next *character* in the text, and does the same thing. Not very helpful for a scenario like in Rows 21 and 22, but very nice for Rows 18 and 20, especially if you referenced a cell range for your delimiters. Like this:

$$=TEXTAFTER(A28,\$D\$28:\$D\$30)$$

where the delimiter values are in Cells D28 to D30 instead of listed directly in the function.

If I had a really long list of data entries I was working with, that included a variety of currency symbols, I'd probably use LEFT to extract them from all my entries, and then Remove Duplicates to create a unique list of the currency symbols in my data, that I could then reference with my TEXTAFTER formula.

(Of course, then we have to pause and ask why we're doing that, because if you are going to add those numbers together, that would be a very bad idea. You'd still need them to be separated by currency type because you can't just add USD, BRL, JPY, etc. values to one another without converting everything to one currency. Right? Right.)

The IFS Function

Notation: IFS(logical_test1, value_if_true1,…)

Excel Definition: Checks whether one or more conditions are met and returns a value corresponding to the first TRUE condition.

Technically, the IFS function can completely replace the IF function, but I still prefer to use IF for simple THIS-or-THAT comparisons. Where IFS really shines is when applied to multi-step IF-THEN-ELSE IF-THEN-ELSE type analysis.

The notation only shows you two inputs for IFS: what question you're asking (logical_test1) and the value if that's true (value_if_true1), but for me it really takes more inputs than that to do what I do with IF or IFS.

Let's go back to that first IF example we had where we wanted to keep a cell blank when there was no number to divide by.

Here it is:

$$=IF(C1="","",B1/C1)$$

Take a moment and try to think how you could convert that to an IFS function. According to the notation there, you only need two inputs:

$$=IFS(C1="","")$$

That is a working function. You will get a result. But there's no calculation. Could you get it to do a calculation with just two inputs?

Maybe one of these works:

$$=IFS(C1<>0,B1/C1)$$

$$=IFS(NOT(ISBLANK(C1)),B1/C1)$$

33

The first one is saying that if Cell C1 is not equal to zero, do your calculation. The second uses two functions we haven't covered yet. It basically says that if Cell C1 is not blank then do the calculation. Problem is, both of those return #N/A when Cell C1 doesn't have a value in it.

So really, not what I want. To use IFS in the way I want, I need to give Excel more.

When you add one more comma to one of these IFS functions, Excel's going to show you that you need to start adding additional inputs in pairs:

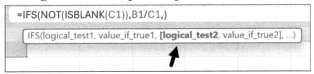

It puts logical_test2, value_if_true2 in the same set of brackets. Meaning if you add one, you have to add the other.

So how would you do that. Because all we really wanted was to do the calculation, right? We wanted to take this

$$=IFS(C1="","")$$

and add one more input for the calculation, but it wants two inputs.

(Do you hate me yet for not just explaining? Yeah, sorry. Trying to keep you awake.)

Here's the answer:

$$=IFS(C1="","",TRUE,B1/C1)$$

We add a new test that you can't fail. TRUE. TRUE is TRUE. And if that's the case, then do the calculation.

So we end up with a formula that basically says, "If Cell C1 is blank, then return a blank value, otherwise, if TRUE is TRUE, which it always is, divide the value in Cell B1 by the value in Cell C1."

I made you walk through this thought process in the hopes that it would stick better for you, because I do not find it intuitive. I always need to remember that my last input is not just, "do the thing", it's a final test that can't be failed, and *then* "do the thing".

You may be wondering why Excel does this. Can't they just default it somehow? And maybe they could've if they'd listed "final result" as the *second* input, but they didn't build it that way. It probably would've been a little counterintuitive. So you have to put TRUE (or some other test that can't be failed) as your final logical test to let Excel know you're done.

Just for kicks, I just tried setting the last test to 2=2, like so:

$$=IFS(C1="","",2=2,B1/C1)$$

and that worked, too.

Excel doesn't know how long your decision tree is, so that final logical test is how you stop.

If you don't give the IFS function a stopping point and none of your prior criteria are met, you'll get a #N/A error message.

Okay, you probably hate IFS right now. But let's go back to our complicated nested IF function and replace it with an IFS function. For those of you who skipped that section, don't worry, just notice how complex this is and that it uses three different IF functions nested together to get results:

$$=IF(\$A8<\$A\$2,\$A8,IF(\$A8<\$A\$3,\$A8*(1-\$B\$2),IF(\$A8<\$A\$4,\$A8*(1-\$B\$3),\$A8*(1-\$B\$4))))$$

Here is that discount table but now using IFS to calculate discounts:

	A	B	C	D	E
1	**Purchase Amount**	**Discount Percent**			
2	$25.00	10%			
3	$50.00	20%			
4	$75.00	25%			
5					
6					
7	**Customer Purchases**	**Price after Discount**			**Formula**
8	$25.00	$22.50			=IFS($A8<$A$2,$A8,$A8<$A$3,$A8*(1-$B$2),$A8<$A$4,$A8*(1-$B$3),TRUE,$A8*(1-$B$4))
9	$50.00	$40.00			=IFS($A9<$A$2,$A9,$A9<$A$3,$A9*(1-$B$2),$A9<$A$4,$A9*(1-$B$3),TRUE,$A9*(1-$B$4))
10	$75.00	$56.25			=IFS($A10<$A$2,$A10,$A10<$A$3,$A10*(1-$B$2),$A10<$A$4,$A10*(1-$B$3),TRUE,$A10*(1-$B$4))
11	$15.00	$15.00			=IFS($A11<$A$2,$A11,$A11<$A$3,$A11*(1-$B$2),$A11<$A$4,$A11*(1-$B$3),TRUE,$A11*(1-$B$4))
12	$60.00	$48.00			=IFS($A12<$A$2,$A12,$A12<$A$3,$A12*(1-$B$2),$A12<$A$4,$A12*(1-$B$3),TRUE,$A12*(1-$B$4))
13	$80.00	$60.00			=IFS($A13<$A$2,$A13,$A13<$A$3,$A13*(1-$B$2),$A13<$A$4,$A13*(1-$B$3),TRUE,$A13*(1-$B$4))
14	$40.00	$36.00			=IFS($A14<$A$2,$A14,$A14<$A$3,$A14*(1-$B$2),$A14<$A$4,$A14*(1-$B$3),TRUE,$A14*(1-$B$4))
15					

And here is the formula for Row 8. Still lengthy, but much easier to write. Let's walk through it.

$$=IFS(\$A8<\$A\$2,\$A8,\$A8<\$A\$3,\$A8*(1-\$B\$2),\$A8<\$A\$4,\$A8*(1-\$B\$3),TRUE,\$A8*(1-\$B\$4))$$

First, let's remove all the dollar signs, which only matter if you want to copy it:

$$=IFS(A8<A2,A8,A8<A3,A8*(1-B2),A8<A4,A8*(1-B3),TRUE,A8*(1-B4))$$

Step one of the formula asks a question:

$$IFS(A8<A2$$

Is the value in Cell A8 less than the value in Cell A2?
Step two tells you what to do if the answer is Yes:

$$A8$$

Return the full customer purchase price from Cell A8.
That's pretty much what the IF function version does, too.

Step three is where things get simpler. Instead of using another IF function, we can just ask another question:

$$A8<A3$$

Is the value in A8 less than the value in A3?
The task to perform if that's the case is:

$$A8*(1-B2)$$

Apply the discount percent in Cell B2 to the value in Cell A8.
Next up is another question and task if true:

$$A8<A4,A8*(1-B3)$$

Is the value in Cell A8 less than the value in Cell A4? Apply the discount in Cell B3 if so.

And then our final question and task if true, which it better be, because our question was the answer, TRUE:

$$TRUE,A8*(1-B4)$$

Apply the highest discount to all remaining purchases.

I know it still feels complex to walk through an example like this, but trust me when I tell you it's much easier to write it.

If you ever get stuck with IFS, it's probably going to be because you asked the wrong questions or told Excel to perform the wrong tasks (rather than a missing paren or comma which is often the issue with IF). So if you aren't getting the right result, draw it out and replace the questions with the cell references that ask the questions.

Like so:

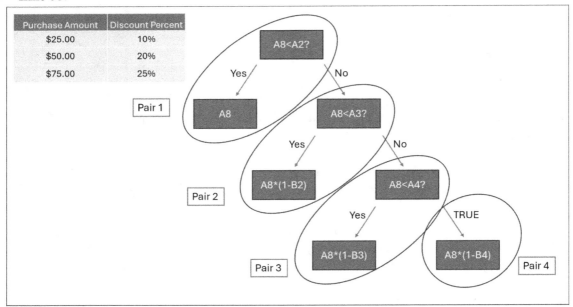

You can then check your IFS function against each paired set, circled in the diagram above.

The XLOOKUP Function

Notation: XLOOKUP(lookup_value, lookup_array, return_array, [if_not_found], [match_mode], [search_mode])

Excel Definition: Searches a range or an array for a match and returns the corresponding item from a second range or array. By default, an exact match is used.

I love this function so much I'm pretty sure I proposed marriage to whoever created it in one of my books. (Not seriously, of course. That would be the bad kind of weird and none of us want to be that.)

Anyway. XLOOKUP lets you take a value, the lookup_value, and then look in a range of cells, the lookup_array, to return a result from a designated range of cells that match up to the lookup array, the return_array.

Your lookup array and your return array can be the same, but they will often be different. For example, you'll look up customer number and want to return customer name.

The other inputs into the XLOOKUP function are optional. They let you tell Excel what to do if there is no match found, whether to match exactly or find the closest result (which is often helpful when you use the same lookup and return array), and how to search.

This is a newer function, so a lot of people aren't using it yet. You may instead stumble upon the VLOOKUP function, which I'll cover in the next chapter. But trust me when I tell you, that this is the function you want to use if at all possible.

Okay. So examples.

Let's start with an exact match example. Here is a table of customer transaction information:

	A	B	C	D	E
1	**Date**	**Customer**	**Product**	**Units**	**Total Cost**
2	2/6/2020	123456	Widget	14	$ 31.50
3	2/25/2020	78542	Whatchamacallit	3	$ 33.75
4	4/1/2020	698124	Widget	8	$ 18.00
5	4/7/2020	12793	Whatchamacallit	11	$ 123.75
6	4/25/2020	3267	Whatsit	11	$ 14.85
7	4/28/2020	4937	Widget	9	$ 20.25

Who is customer 78542? We can go manually look in our customer data table to see it's Shane Morales:

	G	H	I
1	**Customer Number**	**Customer Last Name**	**Customer First Name**
2	3267	Gutierrez	Luisa
3	4937	Holsen	Gary
4	12793	Phong	Bob
5	78542	Morales	Shane
6	123456	Lee	John
7	698124	Jones	Sheila

But what if we want to do this for a thousand transactions? That would be annoying. That's where XLOOKUP can come in handy. We can take the customer number in the first table, look it up in the second table, and then pull the first and last name of each customer. Let's build this for first name.

The first input is what we are looking up.

I want to look up the customer account number in Cell B2, so I start with:

=XLOOKUP(B2,

Next, where am I looking for this?

In my case, all of my information is in the same worksheet and the customer information table has account numbers in Column G, so I can write:

=XLOOKUP(B2,G:G,

If it were in a different worksheet, I'd just go to that worksheet and click on the column that had customer number in it and end up with something like

=XLOOKUP(B2,'Customer Data'!G:G,

The next input is what information we want to pull. First name results are in Column I for me, so that's what I'll use. I could stop there. Everything past that point is optional and I'm okay with the defaults. That would get me:

=XLOOKUP(B2,G:G,I:I)

But let's keep going.

The next input is what to put if there is no listing for what you're looking for. The default is to return #N/A. If you want it to return text, put the text in quotes. Like so:

=XLOOKUP(B3,G:G,I:I,"Unknown Customer Number")

This would return the text "Unknown Customer Number" if there wasn't an exact match between the number I'm looking up and the table I'm looking in.

The next optional input is match_mode. You have four options. If you use zero, 0, Excel looks for an exact match. This is the default option. Your other match choices are -1, which looks for an exact match but will go to the next smaller item in the list if there is no exact match, 1, which looks for an exact match but will go to the next higher item in the list if there isn't an exact match, and 2, which is a wildcard character match.

To use 2, the lookup value you use needs to contain a * or ? wildcard. If I looked for "*Jones", this would tell Excel to match to something like "A Jones".

(Also, just a note as I was playing with this, that Excel treated "Jones" and "Jones " the same for search purposes. It didn't treat that extra space as making the value different. It seems sometimes Excel does and sometimes it doesn't, so you kind of have to test it for search, filter, or functions.)

Okay, so in this instance we want an exact match. We could just put a comma and no number or we can put 0.

=XLOOKUP(B3,G:G,I:I,"Unknown Customer Number",0)

The final input is how to search the list. For an exact match it shouldn't matter what you use.

The two main choices are 1 to search first-to-last and -1 to search last-to-first. Excel does the heavy lifting behind the scenes for those two choices, and puts everything in order for you.

There are other options, but they both require that the lookup_array already be sorted. 2 will search your list assuming the data is sorted in ascending order, and -2 will search assuming the data is sorted in descending order. Do not use them if your data is not sorted properly, and you're trying to find the closest value. You will get an incorrect result.

One more really cool thing to share, and then we'll do a more complex example:

You can have Excel return more than one value at a time for you. For example, in my advertising spreadsheet I have Excel look up the title of my book in a list that then lets it return the author name, the series name, and the official identifier for that book. I used to use three separate formulas to do this, but with XLOOKUP I can do it with one.

Let's go back to our example above:

$$=XLOOKUP(B2,G:G,I:I)$$

If I wanted to return both last name and first name from our customer table at the same time, I would simply list the column range as my last input:

$$=XLOOKUP(B2,G:G,H:I)$$

That assumes, of course, that I want Column H returned before Column I. If I want Column I first and then Column H, I couldn't use this trick, I'd need separate formulas for each lookup array. (And I did try curly brackets on this one and they won't work. So your columns have to be in the same order or you have to write the formulas one lookup array at a time.)

Okay.

Now let's go through an example where we don't want an exact match by revisiting the discount table we used for the IFS function.

I had to make one edit, which was to add a row for no discount. Here we go:

	A	B	C	D	E
1	**Purchase Amount**	**Discount Percent**			
2	$0.00	0%			
3	$25.00	10%			
4	$50.00	20%			
5	$75.00	25%			
6					
7					
8	**Customer Purchases**	**Price after Discount**		**Formula**	
9	$25.00	$22.50		=$A9*(1-XLOOKUP($A9,$A$2:$A$5,$B$2:$B$5,,-1,1))	
10	$50.00	$40.00		=$A10*(1-XLOOKUP($A10,$A$2:$A$5,$B$2:$B$5,,-1,1))	
11	$75.00	$56.25		=$A11*(1-XLOOKUP($A11,$A$2:$A$5,$B$2:$B$5,,-1,1))	
12	$15.00	$15.00		=$A12*(1-XLOOKUP($A12,$A$2:$A$5,$B$2:$B$5,,-1,1))	
13	$60.00	$48.00		=$A13*(1-XLOOKUP($A13,$A$2:$A$5,$B$2:$B$5,,-1,1))	
14	$80.00	$60.00		=$A14*(1-XLOOKUP($A14,$A$2:$A$5,$B$2:$B$5,,-1,1))	
15	$40.00	$36.00		=$A15*(1-XLOOKUP($A15,$A$2:$A$5,$B$2:$B$5,,-1,1))	
16					

That's a lot to absorb. Let's look at the formula in Row 9:

$$=\$A9*(1-XLOOKUP(\$A9,\$A\$2:\$A\$5,\$B\$2:\$B\$5,,-1,1))$$

Those dollar signs are all there to fix cell references to make it easy to copy, so let's take them out for now:

$$=A9*(1-XLOOKUP(A9,A2:A5,B2:B5,,-1,1))$$

Real quick, I want to show you what happens when I replace the entire XLOOKUP function with X:

$$=A9*(1-X)$$

So what this is really doing is having XLOOKUP pull a discount percentage for us. Great. How is it doing that?

$$XLOOKUP(A9,A2:A5,B2:B5,,-1,1)$$

The first input, what to look up, is Cell A9. That's the customer's purchase price.

The next input is our lookup array, Cells A2 through A5. Those are the dollar values for the discount thresholds. Think about that one for a moment. We're not going to have exact matches to those values most of the time. So how would you use those cutoffs? (Hold that thought for now.)

The third input, is our return array, Cells B2 through B5. So we're pulling the discount percentages based on the discount thresholds.

With me so far?

The next input is blank. That's what we'd return if there was a failed lookup. I don't expect to have that, so I'm fine with a default #N/A error message. (Which did happen the first time I ran this. Because I'd forgotten to add that Row 2 that has 0 and 0% and it's needed for this to work.)

The fifth input is very important. I used -1.

That says, "Look for my purchase price. If you can't find an exact match to the purchase price, then drop back to the next lowest value."

So if I have $37.50, I want Excel to drop back to the discount percent for $25. We didn't reach the $50 discount level, we have to go back to the one we did reach.

I used 1 for the final input here, but I didn't need it. My data is sorted in ascending order, so the only option that wouldn't work is -2.

Excel went through for each of my values, looked for the customer's purchase price, compared it to the discount table, and gave the discount percent that the customer had reached. I needed that $0 level for it to have somewhere to drop back to when a customer hadn't reached the first discount threshold.

Great, so that worked.

But where I think XLOOKUP really shines, is with data that is messier. Let's look at an example.

In the table on the next page, Rows 1 through 9 are our data set, which contains information about different books, author, series, title, wordcount, hours to write, and genre.

The unique value that we can look up, Title, is in Column C. There can be duplicates in the other columns, such as author name or series name, but there is only one example of each Title in this table.

I want to look for author name (in Column A) and series (in Column B) for each title. How would you do that?

You can see how I did it in Rows 12 through 14. The formula I used for Title H is in Row 12:

$$=XLOOKUP(A12,C2:C9,A2:B9,,0,1)$$

	A	B	C	D	E	F
1	Author Name	Related Series	Title	Wordcount	Hours to Write	Genre
2	Author A	Series A	Title A	26,527	26.5	Non-Fiction
3	Author A	Series C	Title C	7,893	6	Non-Fiction
4	Author A	Series C	Title E	4,997	4	Non-Fiction
5	Author A	Series C	Title F	7,976	4.25	Non-Fiction
6	Author A	Series C	Title G	57,900	23	Non-Fiction
7	Author A	Series A	Title H	8,284	5.75	Non-Fiction
8	Author B	Series B	Title B	46,204	54.25	Spec Fiction
9	Author B	Series B		6,079	4	Spec Fiction
10						
11	Value	Formula			Result	
12	Title H	=XLOOKUP($A12,$C$2:$C$9,$A$2:$B$9,,0,1)			Author A	Series A
13	Title E	=XLOOKUP($A13,$C$2:$C$9,$A$2:$B$9,,0,1)			Author A	Series C
14	Title B	=XLOOKUP($A14,$C$2:$C$9,$A$2:$B$9,,0,1)			Author B	Series B
15						

That says, look for the value in Cell A12, Title H, in Cells C2 through C9. When you find an exact match, pull the values in Columns A and B from the same row.

Because I wanted it to return results from both Columns A and B, the results show up in Cells E12 *and* F12. Cell E12 is where the actual formula that returns that result is. Since this is an array result, I would see a #SPILL! error in Cell E12 if there was already something in Cell F12.

One final cool thing that XLOOKUP can do (and that I always forget about), is return results between two points. If you combine it with SUM, it can return the sum of the result for a range of cells.

Here we go:

	A	B	C	D	E	F	G	H
1		Units Sold		Start	End	Formula	Result	
2	January	1,253		January	March	=XLOOKUP(D2,$A$2:$A$13,$A$2:$B$13):XLOOKUP(E2,$A$2:$A$13,$A$2:$B$13)	January	1253
3	February	1,417					February	1417
4	March	1,406					March	1406
5	April	929						
6	May	850		January	March	=SUM(XLOOKUP(D2,$A$2:$A$13,$A$2:$B$13):XLOOKUP(E2,$A$2:$A$13,$A$2:$B$13))	4076	
7	June	965						
8	July	736						
9	August	660						
10	September	710						
11	October	1,041						
12	November	942						
13	December	1,159						
14								

Columns A and B have total units sold for each month for a year. Column A has the month, Column B has the number of units sold.

In Rows 2 through 4 of Columns G and H, I have sales results for January, February, and March. These are there as the result of the XLOOKUP function you can see in Cell F2 that was used in Cell G2.

Let's look at it in closer detail:

=XLOOKUP(D2,$A$2:$A$13,$A$2:$B$13):XLOOKUP(E2,$A$2:$A$13,$A$2:$B$13)

That looks complicated, but split it at the colon and you get two XLOOKUP functions:

XLOOKUP(D2,$A$2:$A$13,$A$2:$B$13)

XLOOKUP(E2,$A$2:$A$13,$A$2:$B$13)

One is looking up the value in Cell D2, which is January. The other is looking up the value in Cell E2, which is March. That colon is basically saying "through".

So Excel pulls the results not just for January and March, but for any months between them. In this case, just February, and returns an array result in Cells G2 through H4.

In Cell G6, I took that formula and wrapped it inside a SUM function. You can see the formula I used in Cell F6:

=SUM(XLOOKUP(D2,$A$2:$A$13,$A$2:$B$13):XLOOKUP(E2,$A$2:$A$13,$A$2:$B$13))

Once more, it looks messy, but it's basically

=SUM(X)

Where X is the individual results from the XLOOKUP functions we just discussed, which returned the number of units sold for January *through* March.

Pretty cool, huh?

One more for you:

	A	B	C	D	E	F	G	H
1		Units Sold		Start	End	Formula	Result	
2	January	1,253		January	December	=XLOOKUP(D2,$A$2:$A$13,$A$2:$B$13):XLOOKUP(E2,$A$2:$A$13,$A$2:$B$13)	January	1253
3	February	1,417					February	1417
4	March	1,406					March	1406
5	April	929					April	929
6	May	850					May	850
7	June	965					June	965
8	July	736					July	736
9	August	660					August	660
10	September	710					September	710
11	October	1,041					October	1041
12	November	942					November	942
13	December	1,159					December	1159
14								
15				January	December	=SUM(XLOOKUP(D2,$A$2:$A$13,$A$2:$B$13):XLOOKUP(E2,$A$2:$A$13,$A$2:$B$13))	12068	
16								

All I did here was change the value in Cell E2 to December instead of March, and Excel pulled results for January *through* December.

Now, this worked because I have my months in the correct order. But if I move December to Cell A4, then Excel will stop at that point and not keep going. Using the colon basically says "pull the result for this first value and keep pulling results until you pull the result for the second value."

Appendix A: Basic Terminology

Workbook

A workbook is what Excel likes to call an Excel file.

Worksheet

Excel defines a worksheet as the primary document you use in Excel to store and work with your data. A worksheet is organized into Columns and Rows that form Cells. A workbook can contain multiple worksheets.

Columns

Excel uses columns and rows to display information. Columns run across the top of the worksheet and, unless you've done something funky with your settings, are identified using letters of the alphabet.

The first column in a worksheet will always be Column A. And the number of columns in your worksheet will remain the same, regardless of how many columns you delete, add, or move around. Think of columns as location information that is actually separate from the data in the worksheet.

Rows

Rows run down the side of each worksheet and are numbered starting at 1 and up to a very high number. Row numbers are also locational information. The first row will always be numbered 1, the second row will always be numbered 2, and so on and so forth. There will also always be a fixed number of rows in each worksheet regardless of how many rows of data you delete, add, or move around.

Cells

Cells are where the row and column data comes together. Cells are identified using the letter for the column and the number for the row that intersect to form that cell. For example, Cell A1 is the cell that is in the first column and first row of the worksheet.

Click

If I tell you to click on something, that means to use your mouse (or trackpad) to move the cursor on the screen over to a specific location and left-click or right-click on the option. If you left-click, this selects the item. If you right-click, this generally displays a dropdown list of options to choose from. If I don't tell you which to do, left- or right-click, then left-click.

Left-click/Right-click

If you look at your mouse you generally have two flat buttons to press. One is on the left side, one is on the right. If I say left-click that means to press down on the button on the left. If I say right-click that means press down on the button on the right.

Select

If I tell you to "select" cells, that means to highlight them. You can either left-click and drag to select a range of cells or hold down the Ctrl key as you click on individual cells. To select an entire column, click on the letter for the column. To select an entire row, click on the number for the row.

Data

Data is the information you enter into your worksheet.

Data Table

I may also sometimes refer to a data table or table of data. This is just a combination of cells that contain data in them.

Arrow

If I tell you to arrow to somewhere or to arrow right, left, up, or down, this just means use the arrow keys to navigate to a new cell.

Cursor Functions

The cursor is what moves around when you move your mouse or use the trackpad. In Excel the cursor changes its appearance depending on what functions you can perform.

Tab

I am going to talk a lot about Tabs, which are the options you have to choose from at the top of the workspace. The default tab names are File, Home, Insert, Page Layout, Formulas, Data, Review, View, and Help. But there are certain times when additional tabs will appear, for example, when you create a pivot table or a chart.

(This should not be confused with the Tab key which can be used to move across cells.)

Dropdown Menus

A dropdown menu is a listing of available choices that you can see when you right-click in certain places such as the main workspace or on a worksheet name. You will also see them when you click on an arrow next to or below an option in the top menu.

Dialogue Boxes

Dialogue boxes are pop-up boxes that contain additional choices.

Scroll Bars

When you have more information than will show in a screen, dialogue box, or dropdown menu, you will see scroll bars on the right side or bottom that allow you to navigate to see the rest of the information.

Formula Bar

The formula bar is the long white bar at the top of the main workspace directly below the top menu options that lets you see the actual contents of a cell, not just the displayed value.

Cell Notation

Cells are referred to by their column and row position. So Cell A1 is the cell that's the intersection of the first column and first row in the worksheet.

When written in Excel you just use A1, you do not need to include the word cell. A colon (:) can be used to reference a range of cells. A comma (,) can be used to separate cell references.

When in doubt about how to define a cell range, click into a cell, type =, and then go and select the cells you want to reference. Excel will describe your selection in the formula bar using cell notation.

Paste Special Values

Paste Special Values is a way of pasting copied values that keeps the calculation results or the cell values but removes any formulas or formatting.

Task Pane

On occasion Excel will open a task pane, which is different from a dialogue box because it is part of the workspace. These will normally appear on the right-hand side in Excel for tasks such as working with pivot tables or charts or using the built-in Help function. (They often appear on the left-hand side in Word.)

They can be closed by clicking on the X in the top right corner.

About the Author

M.L. Humphrey is a former stockbroker with a degree in Economics from Stanford and an MBA from Wharton who has spent close to twenty years as a regulator and consultant in the financial services industry.

You can reach M.L. at mlhumphreywriter@gmail.com or at mlhumphrey.com.

* * *

If you want to learn more about Microsoft Excel, check out *Excel Tips and Tricks* or one of the main Excel Essentials titles, such as *Excel 2024 for Beginners*, *Intermediate Excel 2024*, or *Excel 2024 Useful Functions*.

www.ingramcontent.com/pod-product-compliance
Lightning Source LLC
LaVergne TN
LVHW081349050326
832903LV00024B/1372